AN ANTHOLOGY OF INTRIGUING

Animals

POSTER BOOK

DK | Penguin Random House

Acquisitions Editor James Mitchem
Senior Designer Ann Cannings
Editor Becca Arlington
US Senior Editor Shannon Beatty
Jacket Coordinator Magda Pszuk
Jacket Designer Elle Ward
Senior Production Editor Nikoleta Parasaki
Senior Production Controller Ena Matagic
Picture Research Sakshi Saluja
Publishing Director Sarah Larter

First American Edition, 2023
Published in the United States by DK Publishing
1745 Broadway, 20th Floor, New York, NY 10019

Material used in this book was previously published in:
An Anthology of Intriguing Animals (2018)

A catalog record for this book
is available from the Library of Congress.
ISBN: 978-0-7440-9803-7

DK books are available at special discounts when
purchased in bulk for sales promotions, premiums,
fund-raising, or educational use. For details, contact:
DK Publishing Special Markets, 1745 Broadway, 20th
Floor, New York, NY 10019
SpecialSales@dk.com

Printed and bound in China

For the curious
www.dk.com

MIX
Paper | Supporting responsible forestry
FSC™ C018179

This book was made with Forest
Stewardship Council™ certified
paper – one small step in DK's
commitment to a sustainable future.
For more information go to
www.dk.com/our-green-pledge

DK would like to thank the following for their contributions to the
original *An Anthology of Intriguing Animals*: Ben Hoare for the text;
Daniel Long for the animal illustrations; Angela Rizza for the pattern and
foliage illustrations; and Daniela Terrazzini for the cover illustrations.

Picture credits
The publisher would like to thank the following for their kind permission to reproduce their
photographs:
(Key: a-above; b-below/bottom; c-centre; f-far; l-left; r-right; t-top)

3 Dreamstime.com: Yiu Tung Lee. **5 Alamy Stock Photo:** Matthijs Kuijpers. **7 Dreamstime.com:**
Isselee. **9 Fotolia:** anekoho. **11 Alamy Stock Photo:** WaterFrame_mus. **15 123RF.com:** Isselee Eric
Philippe. **17 Alamy Stock Photo:** Frans Lanting Studio. **19 Alamy Stock Photo:** Rachel Rofe. **21
Alamy Stock Photo:** blickwinkel / F. Stober. **23 Getty Images / iStock:** Freder. **27 Alamy Stock
Photo:** Eric Gevaert. **29 Alamy Stock Photo:** Miroslav Valasek. **31 Alamy Stock Photo:** D. Parer &
E. Parer-Cook / Minden Pictures. **33 Alamy Stock Photo:** Zoonar / Daniel Lamborn. **35 Getty
Images:** John Conrad. **37 Alamy Stock Photo:** Nobuo Matsumura. **41 Alamy Stock Photo:** Life on
white. **43 Alamy Stock Photo:** Steve Bloom Images. **45 Alamy Stock Photo:** John Gooday. **47
Alamy Stock Photo:** Picture Partners. **49 Dreamstime.com:** Isselee. **51 Alamy Stock Photo:** Murray
Hayward / All Canada Photos. **53 Alamy Stock Photo:** Thiriet / Andia. **55 Alamy Stock Photo:**
Tomas Rak. **57 Dreamstime.com:** Petergyure. **61 Getty Images / iStock:** 35007. **63 SuperStock:**
Pete Oxford / Minden Pictures

Cover images: *Front:* **Alamy Stock Photo:** Frans Lanting Studio bl, Marco Uliana tc; **Dorling
Kindersley:** Jerry Young c; **Dreamstime.com:** Isselee bc, Petergyure tl, Svetlana Larina / Blair_witch tr;
Andy Morffew: cra; **Photolibrary:** Photodisc / White cla; *Back:* **Fotolia:** anekoho cr

All other images © Dorling Kindersley.

Poster list

Jellyfish · Cobra · Hippopotamus
Peafowl · Baleen whale · Tiger
Kiwi · Zebra · Raccoon
Elephant · Puma · Vulture
Lemur · Pheasant · Marine iguana
Clown fish · Seal · Octopus
Mandrill · Axolotl · Giant panda
Gorilla · Koala · Owl
Sheep · Hedgehog · Wasp
Kingfisher · Bat · Crocodile · Boa

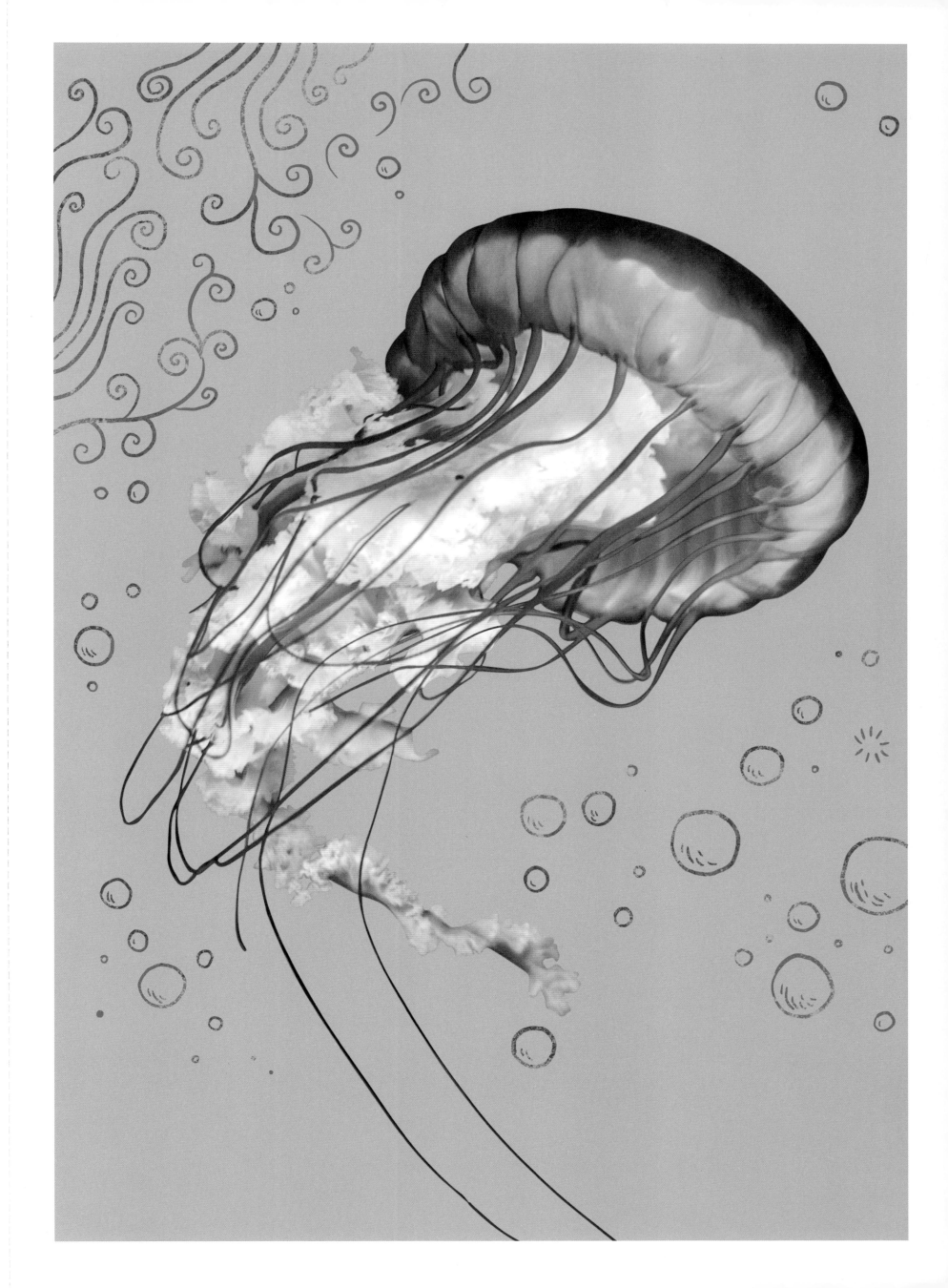

Jellyfish

Jellyfish don't have bones, a brain, or a heart.
They are made up almost entirely of water,
and drift wherever the current takes them.

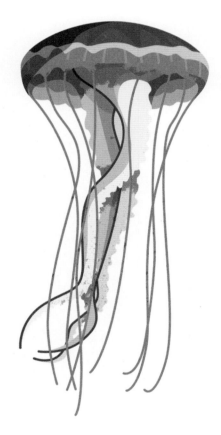

Pacific sea nettle

Chrysaora fuscescens
Group: Invertebrate
Tentacle length: 15 ft (4.6 m)
Location: Eastern Pacific Ocean

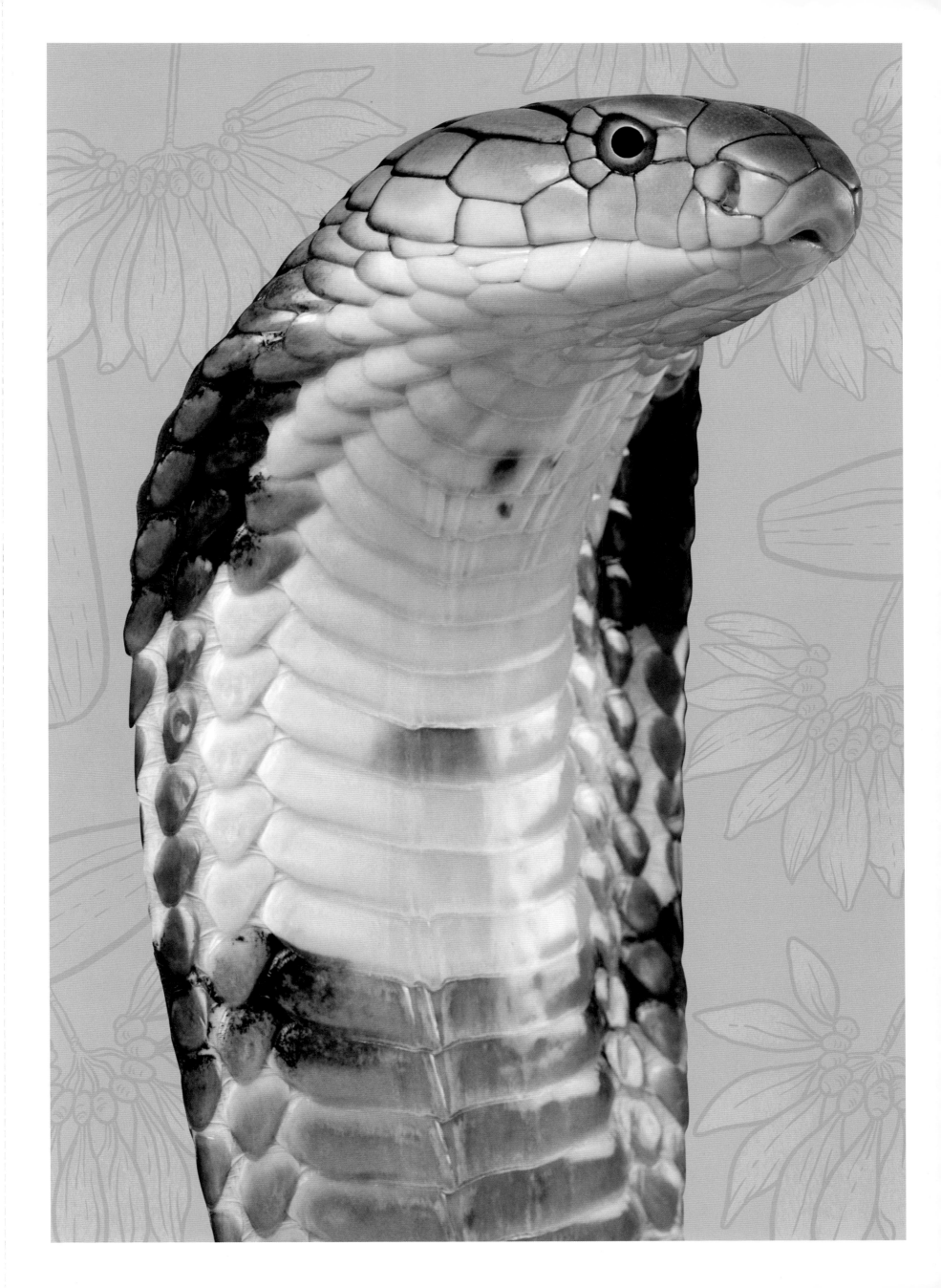

Cobra

The king cobra is the longest venomous snake in the world. Unlike most other snakes, king cobras don't hiss—instead they make a growling sound.

King cobra
Ophiophagus hannah
Group: Reptile
Length: 13 ft (4 m)
Location: Southeast Asia

Hippopotamus

Hippopotamus bathe in muddy water to stay cool in the baking sun. They are notoriously bad-tempered and dangerous if disturbed.

Common hippopotamus
Hippopotamus amphibius
Group: Mammal
Length without tail: 17 ft (5.1 m)
Location: Africa

Peafowl

Male peafowls are called peacocks, and females are called peahens. Peacocks have brightly colored feathers that are used to attract females.

Peacock

Peahen

Indian peafowl
Pavo cristatus
Group: Bird
Length: 11 ft (3.5 m)
Location: Southern Asia

Baleen whale

Baleen whales, such as humpbacks, spend their lives in the ocean. However, they must come to the surface to breathe. To help with this, their nostrils are located on the top of their heads.

Humpback whale
Megaptera novaeangliae
Group: Mammal
Length: 56 ft (17 m)
Location: Worldwide

Tiger

Tigers are the largest and most powerful big cats.
They hunt alone, often at night, taking advantage
of their stripes to blend in with the long grass.

Tiger
Panthera tigris
Group: Mammal
Length: 13 ft (4 m)
Location: Eastern Asia, southern Asia
and Southeast Asia

Kiwi

These round, fluffy, flightless birds are native to New Zealand. They hunt at night, searching for insects by smell and touch.

Northern brown kiwi
Apteryx mantelli
Group: *Bird*
Length: 26 in (65 cm)
Location: North Island of New Zealand

Zebra

Zebras are wild horses, and each one
has a unique pattern in their stripes.
Their hooves are actually huge toenails.

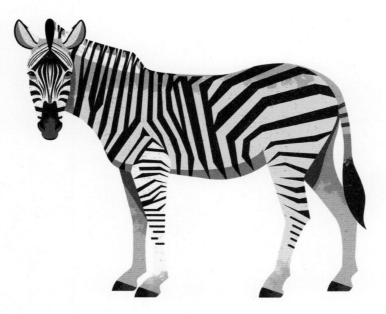

Plains zebra
Equus quagga
Group: Mammal
Length without tail: 8 ft (2.4 m)
Location: Eastern and southern Africa

Raccoon

Raccoons have nimble hands, and can use them to open doors and get inside bins. They used to live in the woods, but are now quite common in towns.

Northern raccoon
Procyon lotor
Group: Mammal
Tentacle length: 3 ft (1 m)
Location: North and Central America

Elephant

When people say elephants never forget, they're not joking—elephants remember other elephants, even if they haven't seen them for years. The heaviest of all land animals, elephants cool off by spraying water on themselves with their trunks.

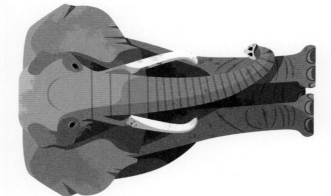

African bush elephant

Loxodonta africana

Group: Mammal

Length with trunk and without tail: 25 ft (7.5 m)

Location: Africa

Puma

Pumas are very elusive and good at hiding, so are rarely seen by humans. They are sometimes called mountain lions or cougars.

Puma
Puma concolor
Group: Mammal
Length: 8 ft (2.5 m)
Location: North, Central, and South America

Vulture

Vultures are scavengers, which means they mostly feast on dead animals. They circle the sky looking for carcasses to eat.

Rüppell's vulture
Gyps rueppelli
Group: Bird
Length: 3 ft (1 m)
Location: Northern and eastern Africa

Lemur

Lemurs are social animals only found on the island of Madagascar. They live in groups of up to 30, and rarely stray far from one another.

Ring-tailed lemur
Lemur catta
Group: Mammal
Length: 4 ft (1.2 m)
Location: Madagascar

Pheasant

Seen as a sign of beauty and luck in their home
of China, golden pheasants live in shady forests.
Males have brightly colored plumage that
helps them attract females.

Golden Pheasant
Chrysolophus pictus
Group: Bird
Length: 4 ft (1.2 m)
Location: China

Marine iguana

Marine iguanas are the only marine lizards in the world. They are only found on the Galápagos Islands, and each island's iguanas are a different color.

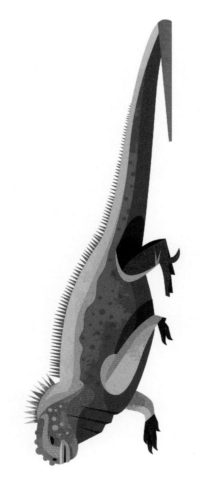

Marine iguana
Amblyrhynchus cristatus
Group: Reptile
Length: 5 ft (1.5 m)
Location: Galápagos Islands off South America

Clown fish

These colorful fish live on coral reefs,
where they take shelter in sea anemones.
The anemones keep the clown fish hidden and
the clown fish keep the anemones clean.

Common clownfish
Amphiprion ocellaris
Group: Fish
Length: 4 in (11 cm)
Location: Eastern Indian and
western Pacific Oceans

Seal

Harp seals are born with fur to keep them warm in their icy environment. They are named for their markings, which look like the musical instrument.

Harp seal
Pagophilus groenlandicus
Group: Mammal
Length: 6 ft (1.7 m)
Location: Arctic Ocean

Octopus

Octopuses are very clever animals. In captivity they have been observed escaping mazes and solving puzzles. They have blue blood, three hearts, and eight limbs.

Common Octopus

Octopus vulgaris

Group: Invertebrate
Length: 4 ft (1.3 m)
Location: Worldwide

Mandrill

Male mandrills are the largest, and one of the most colorful monkeys in the world. Female and young mandrills climb trees, but males are too heavy.

Mandrill
Mandrillus sphinx
Group: Mammal
Length without tail: 4 ft (1.1 m)
Location: Central Africa

Axolotl

Axolotl means "water servant". These strange animals are very rare, and are only found in one lake in the wild. Amazingly, if injured, they can regrow new body parts.

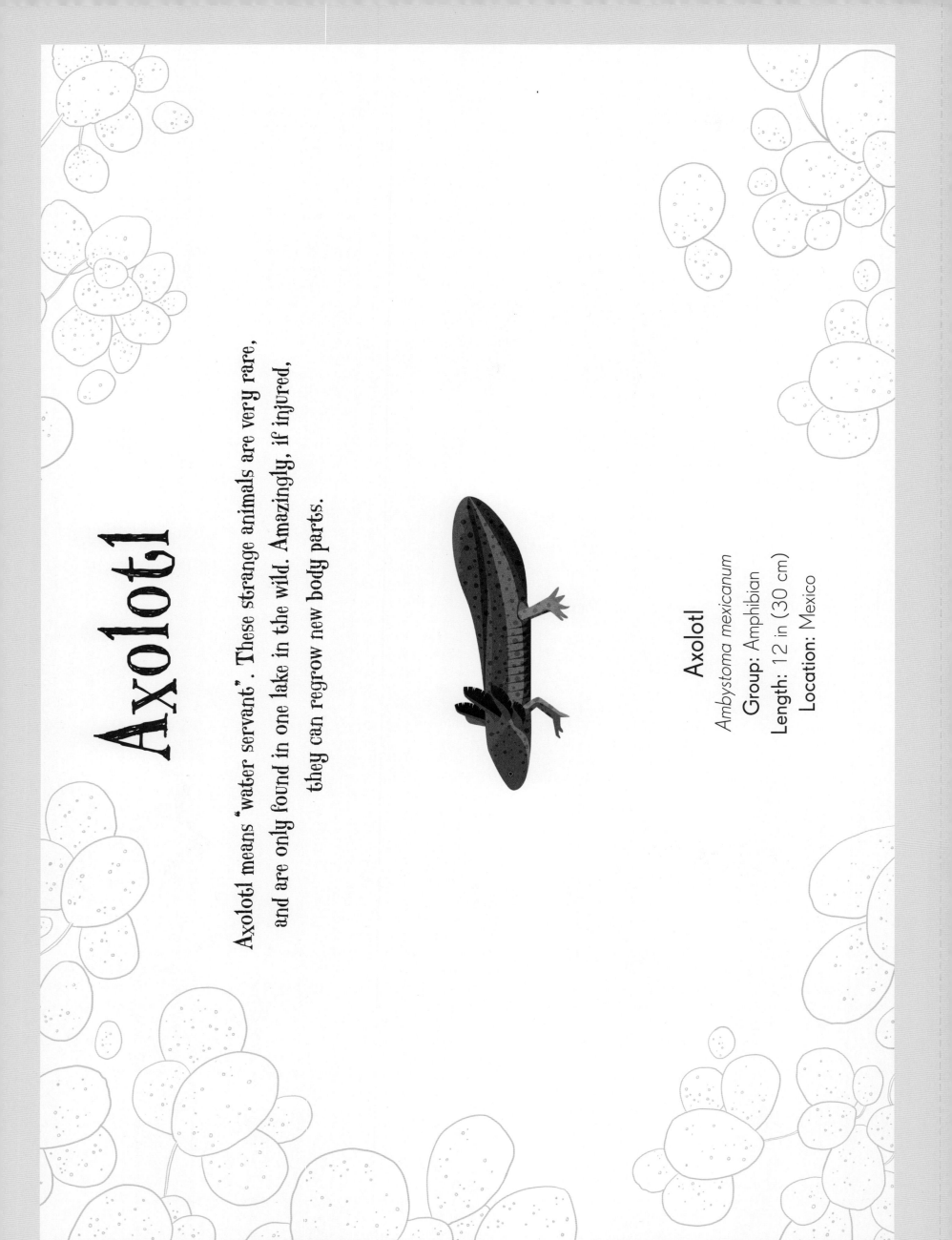

Axolotl

Ambystoma mexicanum

Group: Amphibian

Length: 12 in (30 cm)

Location: Mexico

Giant panda

Called "bamboo bears" by the locals, pandas live in the mountains of China. They spend half of every day eating their favorite food—bamboo.

Giant panda
Ailuropoda melanoleuca
Group: Mammal
Length without tail: 6 ft (1.8 m)
Location: China

Gorilla

Despite their strength, gorillas are gentle giants. They eat enormous amounts of leaves and fruit each day, and baby gorillas enjoy cuddles and piggyback rides!

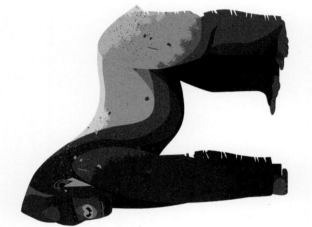

Western gorilla
Gorilla gorilla
Group: Mammal
Height: 6 ft (1.8 m)
Location: Central Africa

Koala

Koalas only eat the leaves of eucalyptus trees, which don't contain much energy. Because of this, koalas sleep or sit for about 20 hours a day.

Koala

Phascolarctos cinereus
Group: Mammal
Length: 32 in (80 cm)
Location: Eastern Australia

Owl

Owls hunt at night. They can't move their eyes, but can twist their heads almost all the way around to spot prey. Owls are often associated with wisdom.

Eurasian eagle owl
Bubo bubo
Group: Bird
Length: 30 in (75 cm)
Location: Europe and Asia

Sheep

There are more than a billion domestic sheep in farms around the world, but wild sheep can live in harsh environments. Bighorn sheep live in the North American mountains. The males use their large horns in head-butting fights.

Bighorn sheep
Ovis canadensis
Group: Mammal
Length without tail: 6 ft (1.7 m)
Location: Western North America

Hedgehog

Hedgehogs have a few special tricks to defend themselves. They are covered in special spiky hairs, and can curl into a ball when they feel threatened.

European hedgehog
Erinaceus europaeus
Group: Mammal
Length without tail: 12 in (30 cm)
Location: Europe

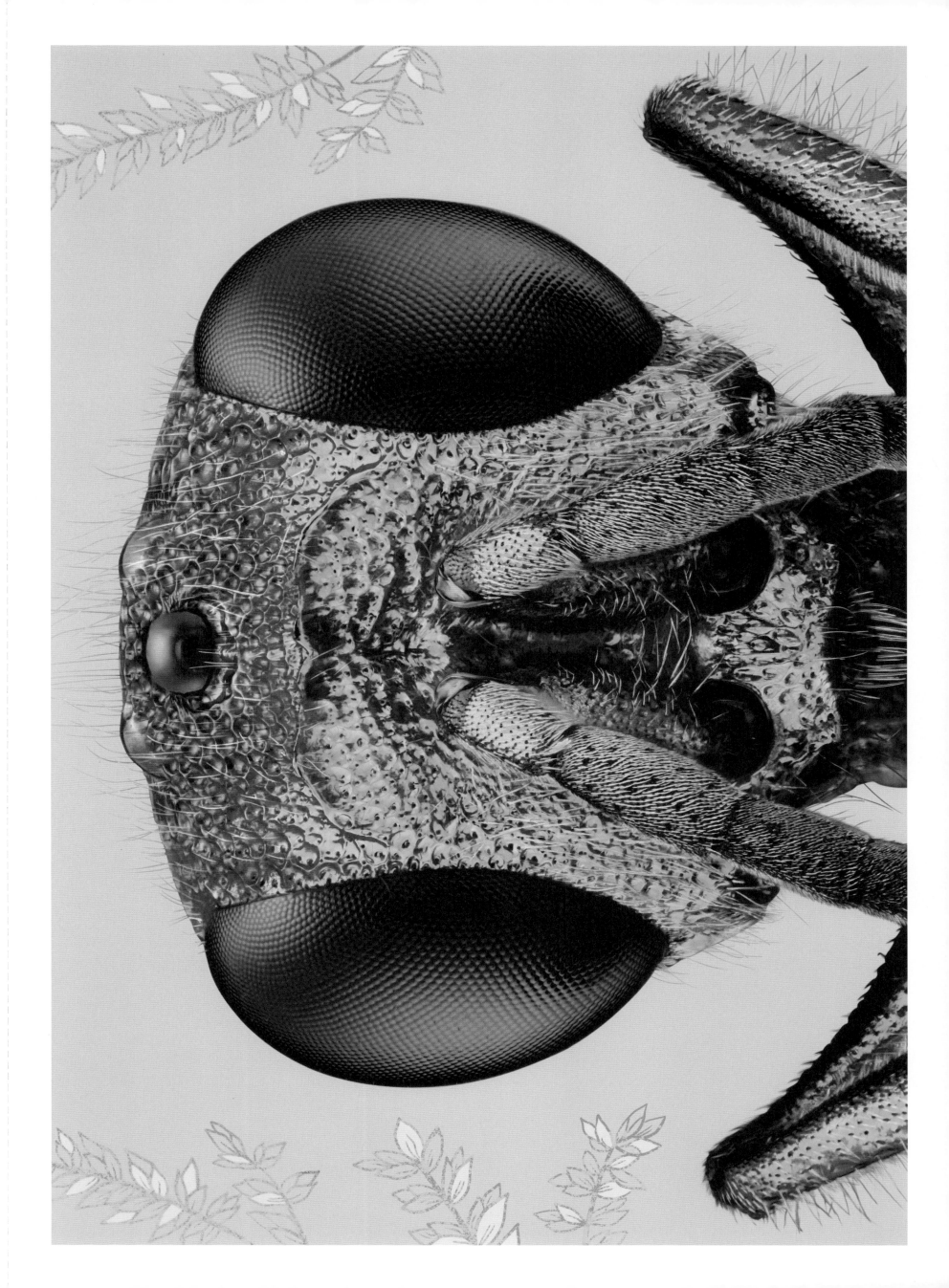

Wasp

Only female wasps have stingers, which they use to kill prey or to defend themselves. Colorful cuckoo wasps are tiny, and are covered in small dimples that protect them from the stings of other insects.

Cuckoo wasp
Holopyga generosa
Group: Invertebrate
Length: ¼ in (0.7 cm)
Location: Europe

Kingfisher

After spotting prey from above, kingfishers dive
into the water to catch fish at incredible speeds.

Common kingfisher
Alcedo atthis
Group: Bird
Length: 6 in (16 cm)
Location: Northern Africa, Europe, and Asia

Bat

Bats are the only mammals that can fly.
Some bats use a special skill called echolocation
to help them hunt in the darkness.

Lyle's flying fox
Pteropus lylei
Group: Mammal
Wingspan: 35 in (90 cm)
Location: Southeast Asia

Crocodile

Saltwater crocodiles are the largest of all reptiles, and most of their time is spent lying in muddy water, waiting for prey. They're not fussy about what they eat, and anything that comes close could be their next meal.

Saltwater crocodile

Crocodylus porosus

Group: Reptile

Length: 23 ft (7 m)

Location: Southeast Asia and Australia

Boa

Boas spend hours looped around tree branches waiting for prey. They kill their prey by squeezing it until it stops moving, then swallow it in a single bite.

Emerald tree boa
Corallus caninus
Group: Reptile
Length: 7 ft (2.2 m)
Location: South America